The Memories We Become

Calvin Beck-Godoy

The Memories We Become

Cover design by Karina Benbow

ISBN: 978-0-646-83910-3

DEDICATION

To my two happy dogs, who sat by my side through the memories I became. Without words, with patience, and unconditional love.

CONTENTS

INTRO

Do we need to think about who we are?

Is it something you consider?

Is it a well-established truth?

Do we perceive ourselves in ever changing perspectives? Do we prescribe a static identity? So sure, this time knowing, this new thing, certain of direction, and why everything has ever happened.

Do we need to form an identity for ourselves or be open to exist moment to moment without firm boundaries? More aware of our reality rather than the ideas we give our perspectives.

Have you embraced that you are the source of your awareness or is that just a given? That you are becoming and what you have become. The transformations we undergo are never the end. They are our very nature.

What have you become?

From which vision, which sensation, which moment did this become your form?

Our childhood is distinctly us even though so much has changed.

But what really changed?

What was given in the memories we became?

OPEN YOUR MIND

Vivid power pulsed through their mind while pondering the final transformation. There was excitement at the conception of the ultimate state of being.

Slowly they began levitating as they filled with what can only be described as the purest energy. Before it could be comprehended it vanished. Something at their base, at the floor of their existence, had been awakened.

This floor cracked and an untameable essence was released. It was set free. All good and evil within the spectrum of humanity began funnelling through. Reality with absolute intensity at the edge of human possibility.

It was sudden but continuous and with it, all individual feeling was gone. There was no more to be felt. Everything that could be felt, was. The most euphoric pleasure and the most wretched pain, both distinct and united at once.

Then began a bubbling growth in size. Rippling at every part of their physical being. No inch left unaffected, nothing to stop this irreversible change. The human form held strong but began to tremble. It was nearing the limit of what this body could handle.

Starting at the fingertips, light began to pierce the skin. Eyelids flashed open as it pierced through their eyes. In this moment there was a sonic boom that echoed across the land.

At a gradually quickening pace, the light began crawling upwards. Consuming them till they appeared bathed in it.

The light dimmed slightly before intensifying once more. The body that once held a mortal, morphed into a blinding flame.

Revealing the dormant god within.

Past conception, it was now reality. The peak of existence met.

There was a moment of silence. A calm self-awareness.

Ultimate power united with existence, and with pure intellect at its disposal… It vanished.

Being transitioned into the final ascension.

Becoming the only existence higher.

That of reality itself.

At one with the infinite intelligence of omniscience and omnipresence.

Beyond space and time.

No longer confined by form.

Now all that was.

One story became them all.

Then a baby was born.

PART I

MORE THAN PHYSICAL

A world in motion, floating.

Where you walk, what you said.

What goes on in your head.

Never happens again.

Once.

Memories, scenes, more than a movie.

More than a series of books.

Life, our lives.

Words try to describe.

How a few select moments look.

Pieces of a puzzle, yet to be completed.

What pieces have you found?

Pieces of your puzzle, all of them needed.

Completion is simply now.

To hope is not to know.

Tension guards the way to grow.

Courage to say, yes or no.

Desires guide us home.

Not scared, anxious.

Unfair, dangerous.

Desperate bred shameless.

A life truly painless.

Joyless.

Freed from perfection.

Revealing the lesson.

Beyond the ideal.

What do you feel?

Write your theory.

Faith and doubt.

Logic and reason.

Grab the shovel, travel slow, build your own road.

On the journey, learning how to make it on our own.

The choice can trap us in the question.

Some things are never known.

Feed your power, feed your flame.

Make your house a home.

Lessons passed down are forever in motion.

Does technology change what your goal is?

Different to locations and periods of time.

The balance of the heart and the mind.

A destination, or a way of life?

Bad thoughts, simply bad thoughts.

Created by a balanced mind, thoughts cared for.

The evil the screens are projecting.

How much death there is.

You feel the effect of this.

A compliment, to be savage.

Emancipation from expression is "fashion."

In a state of war and panic.

How do we calm, how do we manage?

Encouraged to be numb, to never give a fuck.

Pressure from poisoned blades that did not cut.

Do not try to forget what was done.

Man makes mistakes, nature makes none.

Let the tension go as intentions grow up.

Trust the journey of learning and love.

World War III.

The casualties and victories all in our head.
Metaphysical battles we must decide to address.

Losing ourselves selfishly sprinting ahead.

Social creatures, our lives connect.

You must show respect.

To those whose ways should be respected.

Breaking obedience from what I am told;

without the truth known.

Consider all lines then decide on my own.

What do we really know yet?

Why do we believe what they have said?

On unpaved paths away from electric hums.
With squawks and scurries where the river runs.

The crackle of gravel and the sound of my breath.
A dance between being and what to do next.

The inkling to stop at every bush, bird and tree.
When there's more to see.

When I simply be.

The growing heart is tender
In a world of reinforced metal.

But nature breaks the concrete.
Beating as we breathe.

Let it beat strong.
Learn what living means.

To hurt, the burn.
The fire caressed by the rain.

Lava cooled by the sea.

How fertile ground is made.

Clusters of contemplation.
Undecided on decisions I should be making.
I trace its shape and say...
Another day, not today.

As I slowly move away.
Through different shades of grey.

As unclear faced as when I turn away.

The sudden echoing cry when you betray yourself.

The inner voice that speaks sweet and clearly.

Quietly.

"You know who you are.

You know your scars.

The deepest crevice in the caves of your heart.

Too long you have you supressed it.

Left it lying in the dark.

People need connection.

Where does your connection start?

Feel the nameless essence,

of whom you really are."

Always looking for a smile.

What made you want to cry?

A friend asks, 'can I help?'

Your instinct is to lie.

The sudden split, the first break.

From what you think, to what you say.

The step astray, a path you take toward a fateful day.

The day you wonder who you are.

What you suddenly became.

The meaning keeping you in doubt.

If you leave it out, it cannot be found.

The script with substance still relies on the projection.

The energy spent.

The clarity of vision.

What you present.

The strength of the signal.

The flick or the punch.

The nibble or the bite.

The splash or the wave.

The memory made or the vision that fades.

The final moment I saw her living eye.
A memory clashed with its moment in time.

Holding her face.

Holding a place.

Feel the space as it drifts away.

The richness of experience so that now can exist.

Devastated what was for where we now live.

The material that made the memory, never drifts too far.
The energy in the web, of which we are all a part.

In a new state, till it is witness to an open door.
Woven into a new carnation.

New purpose in its form.

Lost till you allow patience.
Become awareness of sensation.

Lodged into excess.

Trapped under folds.

Lacking any essence.

Nothing to hold.

Energy focused on the mind.

Obsessing with the problem.

A slave to any sense of vice.

Pleasure and pain revolving.

Without decision or direction.

Any hole a hole to fall in.

With spirit and actions intertwined.

We calibrate for soaring.

The eclipse begun.

Unknown to eyes, some quickly run.

The rest still, deeply stunned.

Not a typical day or routine situation.

Although confused and afraid they stood firm.

They faced it.

Stories were told of the moon overpowering the sun.

How facing the unknown does not mean you should run.

These brave folk were trusted.

Stories told of the skies when night appeared in the day.

A lesson. Aa test of faith.

Stand strong or leave this place.

Searching for more when you are fine, can trouble the mind.

Mistaking 'good' for a low moment in time.

Food for the mental space.

Colour to clouds emotions create.

The mental pace.

The visions, words, ideas, and memories made.

Physical, emotional, and mental awareness to all that surrounds me.

Sound being.

Who creates meaning?

How long am I centred till I start leaning?

Forget the future.

What is in front of us.

The shapes that surround you.

Up, down, and around you.

How much do you notice until you lose focus?

How much can you notice before you lose focus?

If you are not focused,

does your mind close or open?

The truth does not decay, speak words your way.

How a message is conveyed smoothly grooves through your brain.

Regret suppressed openness.

Get it off your chest.

There was a cold wind before the confession.

With the full story involved it uncovered the lesson.

In the open air it could settle, revealing a message.

A life is finite.

Decide how you spend it.

Wishes for a world beyond the land I currently roam.

To be more, to know more.

Confidence in where my effort should go.

Confidence in my direction.

The process, the edge, the clash of intuition and creation.

The desire for more to exist.

The knowledge we acquire makes us more.

All action makes us more, what more do we wish to be?

The right thing when you want to do right things.

The option speaks but it does not sing.

Edging on the cliff of understanding the message.

What I meant and why I said it.

Answers unknown to me.

Learning as I speak.

Happiness in the shadow under the weight of real pain.

A smile you will remember for the rest of your days.

Pierced, punctured, through its pure rays.

It burnt away all resentment of pure heart ache.

Goodwill grows if you let it grow.

In the cold, in the dark, progress will slow.

Will you assist in growth or give it a limit?

With good intentions it can still be finished.

With or against the stream we row.

When you can, take hold.

If you can't –

let go.

A man against his shadow.

A woman against the mirror.

Where do we look to see clearer?

Heartbeat gone but you feel them.

Memories are not enough when you need them.

Still with parts to play.

Change shape, a different pace.

The feeling doesn't go away.

Look up.

Remember their face.

Curves with words.

Untied until awareness starts to hurt.

Holding back, bring out the mind.

Make memories that prepare us.

Powered by awareness.

Powered by what you eat.

Powered by needs, urge, and passion.

Find balance in pleasure and pain.

God like visions will reign.

With no bias from the temptations outside us.

Without thinking ambition spills.

Can we call it real?

Your scope of reality.

How does it feel?

Distraction is a mountain to hike.

Considering the grand scheme of time.

The 6 millionth millimetre in a few hundred miles.

What is the matter?

What does it matter?

What is a reason to fight?

For your life?

For your son?

For your wife?

For your dreams?

To be crowned King?

To save people you do not know?

To make your body a home?

What is not worth fighting for, should not be died for.

Living for a living, what are you living for?

Find a place to sit.

Rest the eyes.

Relax the shoulders.

Drop the bottom lip.

Release your hands.

Bring them back together.

Bonds that bind us will not hold forever.

The present.

The treasure.

It could have been never.

Standing in a crater, a low you made.

A chance to surrender, change the pace.

Prepare for new growth, true and proud.

Ramps and runways touch the ground.

New perspective, through the clouds.

When you are mindful.

A mind full of now.

If fame is the goal, I question the intention.

The need for recognition.

For endless spending.

Stop looking for the final piece.

In time we make amendments.

Hope is homegrown meals.

Friends on sunny days.

Lost is the need for more, where enough never came.

Acceptance is not simple.

Having compassion for their lies.

Patience gave emotion understanding of the mind.

It is hard for the heart to understand,

how love became fear.

Entered the bond with ease,

not as easy to disappear.

A last resort.

The union strangled by tangled cords.

Set like initials into concrete floors.

Wooden furniture, fake plants.

Food scraps, marching ants.

Sunny day, wearing pants.

Force a smile to average tunes by above average bands.

Empty cans, stray cats, and impulse tats.

Open ended questions where any answer is a trap.

Say it all, risk being appalled.

Or screw tight the cap.

Are you full of shit?

Entranced in any fad.

Too tired for a conversation.

Let's have a chat.

Life is never still.

Change what it does.

There is no end.

Even when you're done.

Once you speak your mind, we find leaks and missing links.

Kicks to fix the kinks, leaves a skull with dints.

Mentor the guide to a perfect life.

Men do chores for their perfect wives.

Metaphorical predictions, roll the dice.

Better alone than controlled each night.

Do a few too many things at any one time.

Too few of those things are ever done right.

Bombarded with notifications.

The risks we should be taking.

The matrix is breaking.

Beyond the mainframe our true selves are waking.

Ancient traditions reanimating.

The sound of the ocean, the sand at my feet.

Where a sense of purpose and lost thoughts meet.

Complete.

A calm home set alight.

Ignited a fire.
You could not fight it.
Flames at their hottest soon start dying.

A place you grew to understand, turned to ash.
A phase, a chapter, time came to pass.

The soil is richer.
Same place but different.

Begin again.

The path walked, now with experience.

The future evermore mysterious.

Remember the goal is the end.

A journeys final step.

What about the rest?
What about the rest?

From the outside, in your mind again.
Actions questioned as their happening.

You seem scared, should we be scared too?

You seem prepared, can we follow you?

Dust in the wind carried a seed.
Right time and place, birthed a tree.

A flower of passion blooms suddenly.

Pollinate your mind.
Will it live or die?

The heart of hearts.
Deepest cave on a forgotten path.

Behind the final door.
A portal through a mirror.

A chance to rise or run and hide.
Weakness could not be clearer.

Drown it out with cries and clowns.
The self has been defeated.

Now a cautionary tale.
Your life's only meaning.

To truly know light.
Instil acceptance of the dark.

Hear what the mind speaks.
Feel what the body asks.

Then be you, exactly who you are.

PART II

YESTERDAY
YOU SAID TOMORROW

You took the pill to get lost in now.

Disconnected, you can't be found.

Just a fool, fooling around.

A wish to swim or drown.

Fulfillment or entertainment.

Static or turning pages.

Act or let the day drift.

What exists without creation?

When you try forgetting.

Bet you will not forget it.

Neglect a piece of yourself.

Something is missing.

In vivid dreams, it will be there.

A cure disguised as venom.

Do not be scared.

Touch scars to sculpt a settling mould.

Know who you are to accept yourself whole.

Pain can enter the most beautiful home.

Into which room are you afraid to go?

Vibrations, sensations.

The wave, aura, pulse.

Pure lust or pure love.

What are you made of?

Conceptualise your energy.

You are not the enemy.

Let intention speak.

Let ideas breathe.

Locked inside, locked in size.

Contained till the tension bites.

Physical pain trapped in shade.

Free the spirit, live your life.

True sight through clarity of mind.

Numb the soul with cheap pleasure.

Silence the call to be better.

Too long I watered weeds in my brain.

They flowered a drive to cower.

The shadows of the night.

The brightness of the light.

Will we choose to hide?

Will we choose to rise?

Perfect is the end.

Life is in your actions.

Imperfect is the journey.

Engage as it happens.

A steppingstone can be a locked cage.

Hesitation stole momentum you gained.

When the journey ends, but you feel the same.

How quickly the problem changed.

Consider what you pull from the past.

Sharpen your blade or hold your stance.

When tension goes deep.

The core thread of your pain.

Burn bright with light.

Reveal your chains.

Unable to relax, get some rest.

Hear your heartbeat in your head.

Not tired when you think about it.

Wide awake when you think about it.

You want to sleep.

But it's not an option.

What will you do?

Stay in bed or get up off it.

The noose hangs and it burns.

A killer turned victim in a matter of words.

A rope is not evil.

Existence and presence.

Give a situation respect, assess it.

Muscles tear as they grow.

But bones should not break.

It can be sad letting go.

With good decisions made.

Never hurts to rethink.

What makes up your day.

Repeating old patterns.

Years got away.

Treated life like a pointless simulation.

Contained within a file.

Lost connection with who you are.

Like deception was in style.

With no faith left.

The last string snapped.

The body collapsed.

Every tile smashed.

The lesson, all that was left.

Experience found in a mosaic of neglect.

Balcony view of the car park.

Tree tops and buildings ahead.

Between the rows of cars.

Withered plants almost dead.

Green, yellow, orange.

Then crunchy brown leaves.

In awe, they continue to fall.

The season of fall leaves.

Old, mouldy concrete slates.

Cities grow more each day.

The colours fade.

The plague is grey.

Strangled minds.
Strangled eyes.
Strangled relationship.

Walking down the hall of a sinking ship.

An inspiring mystery.
What caused this pain and misery?

Was everything made, made to be known?

The darkest, deepest cave.
Completely lost.

All alone.

How much power do we have?

Are we selling ourselves short?

All this freedom, do we need it?

So frequently bored.

Words that truly motivate.

What should we say?

"You should be grateful."

"Take on the day."

Driven to brilliance.

Freed passions of the heart.

Rarely done with empty captions.

Under pictures of an ass.

A changing shape.
An eternal form.
Steady towards.
A sterile horn.

Circuits hacked.
It knows your taste.
The colours that hold your gaze.
The desire becomes haunting.
What knowledge lays in pain?

Believe the stories.
Or learn the demon's name.

Join in the applause, wonder what for.

Action spawned without any thought.

Choose to fight, know the reward.

Pride in the fruits mindfully sought.

In flow with the process.

On the edge of what is.

What comes next?

Are you being patient?

Or waiting?

Anxious or accepting?

Considered or rejected?

Every Saturday night.

Closing the blinds; to the true view of your mind.

We play and pay with money and time.

Those moments are moments for life.

Looking back.

Thinking back.

Looking bad.

Thinking sad.

Pleasure is not a good endeavour.

There is one life, no best life ever.

Punishment can gift a lesson.

Now is here, reveal the present.

Think a little introspective.

The lessons of our lost love.

Did we get them?

Free will.

Choose and do what you want.

Wanting something different to want.

Innately wanting.

One thing over something.

Am I in control of myself or guided by pleasure?

Where will the dopamine fix be better?

Binge.

Food, clothes, porn, drugs, stuff, and shows.

Is this how I want to live?

The music finally switched off.

The subscription finally ran out.

A mind stunted left to rot.

No way to force the smile now.

Neglected potential for too long.

All you forced yourself to like.

You knew it was all wrong.

While friends grew in their lives.

Too serious.

Too uptight.

Growing up.

You feared it.

So, you never did.

Words spoken are noises.

To respond or ignore them are choices.

When words make someone cry.

The ideas may not be why.

Consider their life.

Before your voice arrived.

Fragile ideas make way for strong.

It can be hard to admit you're wrong.

Maybe overthinking is getting in the way.

Making a mess just to complain.

Despair crawls from the shadows.

Bringing pity to myself.

Found in an idle mind.

Create a cry for help.

Find a new perspective, the curtain pushed aside.

This is it; I am certain. We've finally arrived.

Free of all the compulsions that occupy the mind.

Abstracting the world, one impulse at a time.

See the whole mountain and how to get higher.

While burning the dead weight, I was burnt by the fire.

Scars cherished, an honest reminder.

Fruitless desire is the resistance inside us.

Time changes as we grow.

Once unseen, now all we know.

What we do in a minute, what we do in an hour.

Where space and energy have their power.

Where we go will affect this.

All that is, in all directions.

A fight against tiredness.

Coffee and the taurine fight us.

Stayed up late, had a hard day.

Get no sleep so tomorrow feels the same.

Stupid brain, you're insane.

It is not a reward.

Wasting time, staying bored.

Weakening your drive.

Weakening your thoughts.

To say: 'Everything is good.'

Does not make it so.

Truth in the fabric of blanket statements.

What is too objective?

What is too offensive?

Care for what you say.

Calm in your message.

A universe alive inside us.

A search for peace since it cannot find us.

What do you feel from your head?

Lower the pressure the more you express.

Truth in all words honestly said.

Allow the world and mind to connect.

Find the answers, do not stay in the dark.

Because a passive now, is a regretful past.

Naive to the sensations holding me.
A wave of compulsion grows steadily.
Lifetimes getting longer.
Winds getting stronger.

A missed take.
I could see straight.
So it's all clear.

Heart struck.
But held up.
Through actions we heal.

No time constraints.
Let it vibrate.
The feeling is real.

Let the waves.
Turn to ripples.
Karma's lesson revealed.

Reaching for missing pieces in a puddle of tears.
Tangled in self wallow on the foundation of years.

No love is felt, only cursing yourself.
Escaping the hurt, neglects why it's felt.

Eyes only weep purely human pain.
Let regret and shame be washed away.

A vulnerable state, to grow in truth.
Nothing to hide the change in you.

Understanding of love and where lies the pain.
So it can be you when they speak your name.

A bottomless pit is the safest place to be.

Back flip, turn into a better me.

Ketamine an upper, then a downer fiend.

It is not cold, it's primal.

For the feeling, fuck survival.

Breathing is vital.

Balloons, spoons and empty vials.

Mind gone.

Never recall the moment we were most high on.

BPM, hammer bass to the head.

Sirens trigger moments of existential dread.

Dance.
Crash.
Regret.
Repeat.

PART III

TAMING THE HEART
TAKES TWO

Velvets touch when her smile showed.

The warmth of a bonfire afterglow.